PIANO · VOCAL · GUITAR

FIFTY SHADES OF GREY

ISBN 978-1-4950-2332-3

HAL•LEONARD®
CORPORATION
7777 W. BLUEMOUND RD. P.O. BOX 13819 MILWAUKEE, WI 53213

Visit Hal Leonard Online at
www.halleonard.com

I PUT A SPELL ON YOU

Words and Music by
JAY HAWKINS

Moderately slow Blues tempo

Lyrics:

I put a spell on you, _____

Instrumental solo

be - cause _____ you're mine. _____

You bet - ter

stop the thing _____ that you're do - ing. _____ I said a-

watch out, I ain't ly - in'. _____

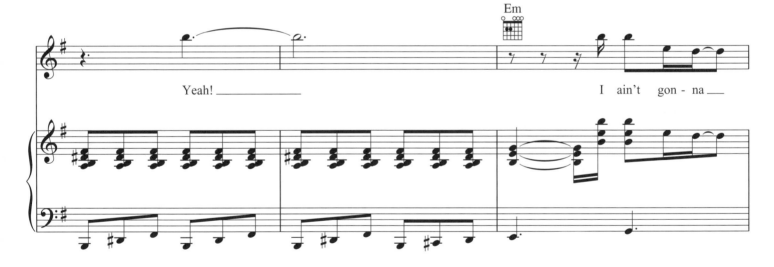

Yeah! _____ I ain't gon - na _____

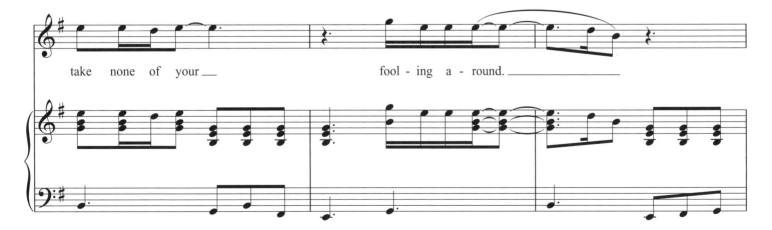

take none of your ____ fool - ing a - round. _____

I ain't gon-na ___ take none of your ___ put-ting me down. ___

I put a spell on you, ___

be - cause ___ you're mine. ___ Whoa whoa,

al - right!

5

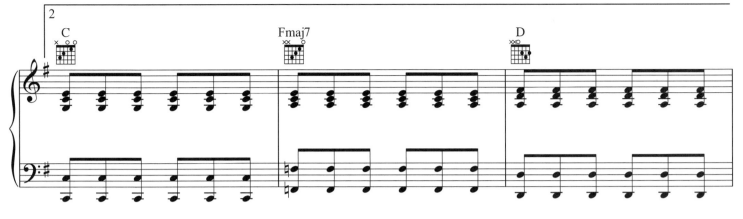

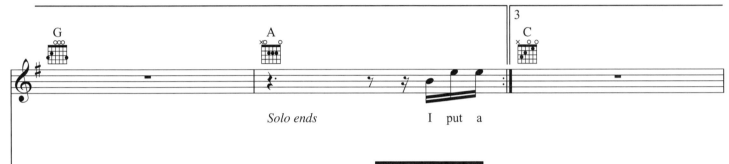

Solo ends   I   put   a

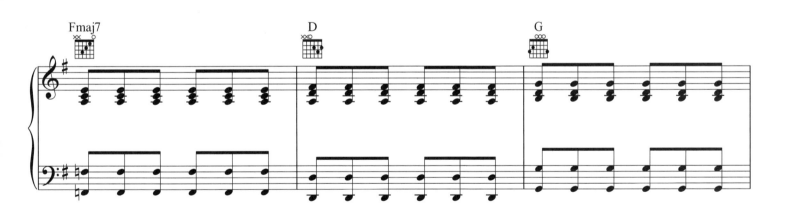

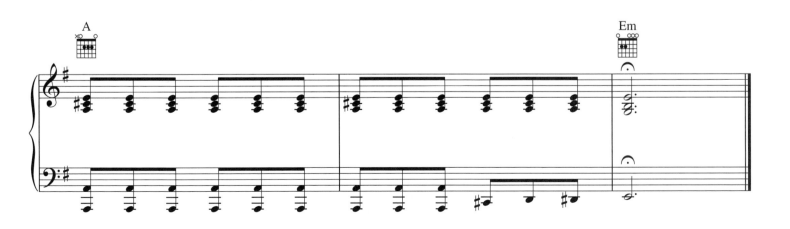

UNDISCOVERED

Words and Music by LAURA WELSH,
AMANDA GHOST, EMILE HAYNIE
and DEVONTE HYNES

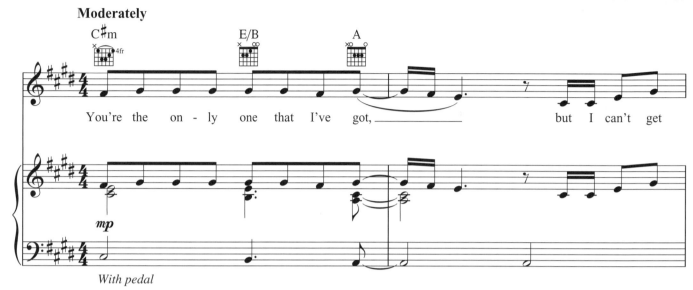

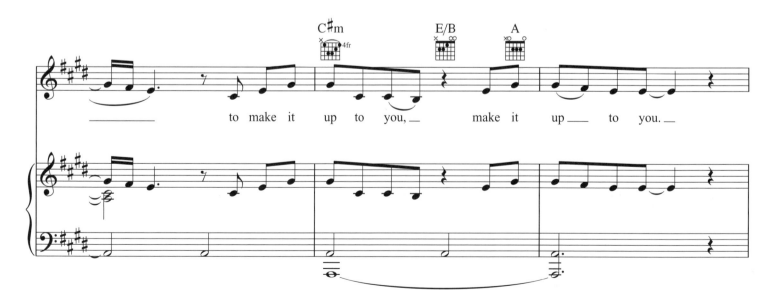

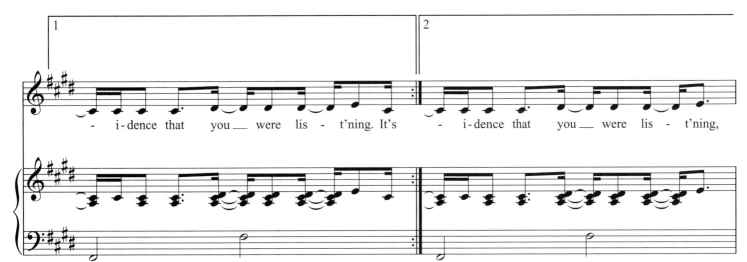

- cov-ered; I wan-na see the rest of you. ___ I can't get next to you, ___ I can't get

next ___ to you. ___ You're un-dis - cov-ered; I wan-na see the rest of you. ___ I can't get

next to you, ___ I can't get next ___ to you. ___ You're un-dis - next ___ to you. ___

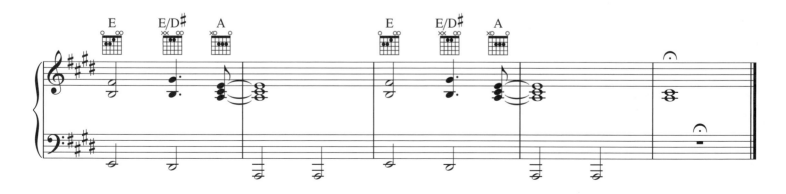

EARNED IT
(Fifty Shades of Grey)

Words and Music by ABEL TESFAYE,
AHMAD BALSHE, STEPHAN MOCCIO
and JASON QUENNEVILLE

hey,   and I'm so used to be - ing used. _____
hey,   you're my fa - v'rite kind __ of   night. _____   So I

love ___ when you call ___ un - ex - pect - ed, ___   'cause I hate ___ when the mo - ment's ex -

pect - ed. ___ So I'm - a care for you, _ you, you.   I'm - a care for ___

you, _ you, you,   yeah, _____   'Cause, girl, you're per - fect,   you're al - ways

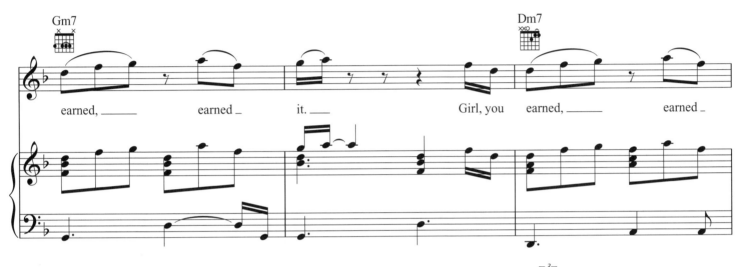

made us be-lieve _ it was on - ly us, con-vinced we were _ bro - ken in -

si - i - i - ide, _ yeah, _ in - si - i - i -

ide. _ Yeah, _ 'cause, girl, you're per - fect; girl, you're per - fect. You're al - ways

worth it, you're al - ways worth ___ it. And you de - serve it, and you de - serve it, the way you

work it, the way you work it. 'Cause, girl, you   earned, _____   earned, _

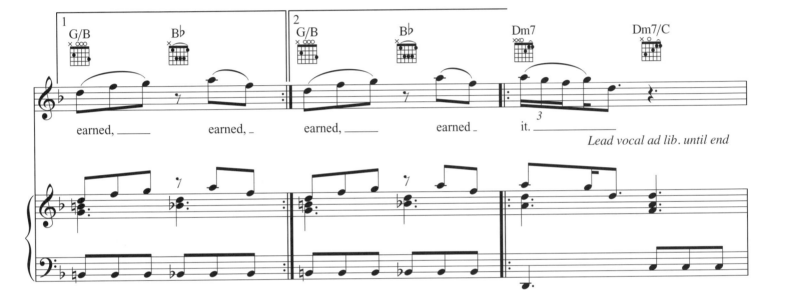

earned, _____   earned, _   earned, _____   earned _   it. _____

Lead vocal ad lib. until end

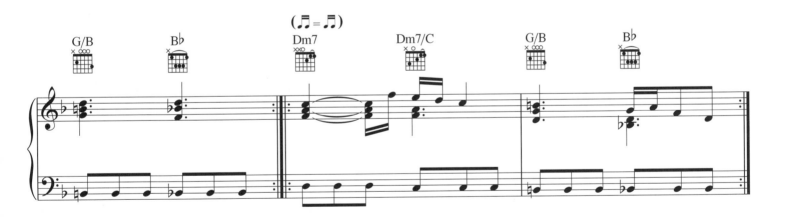

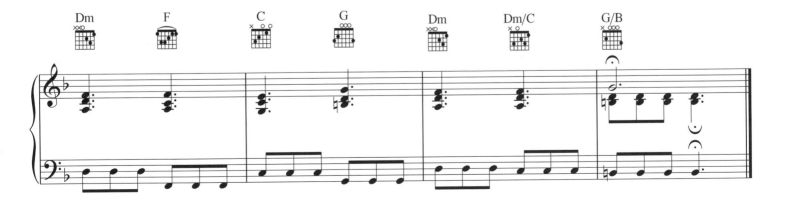

MEET ME IN THE MIDDLE

Words and Music by DAVID OKUMU
and JESSICA WARE

find __ out what took you so long to come back a - round?__ If I'd on - ly been

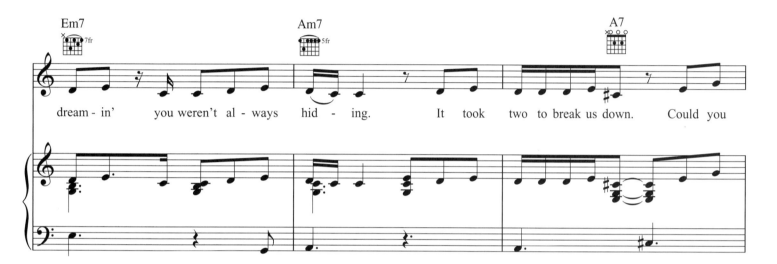

dream - in' you weren't al - ways hid - ing. It took two to break us down. Could you

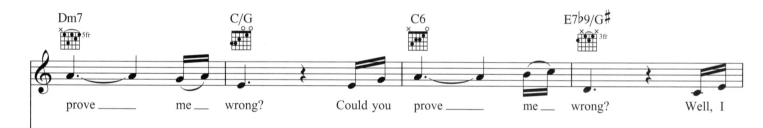

prove _____ me __ wrong? Could you prove _____ me __ wrong? Well, I

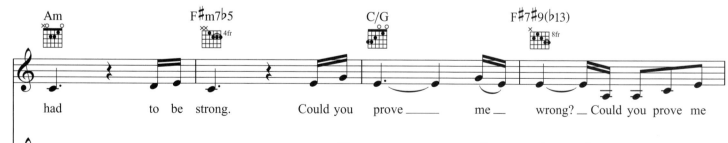

had to be strong. Could you prove _____ me __ wrong? __ Could you prove me

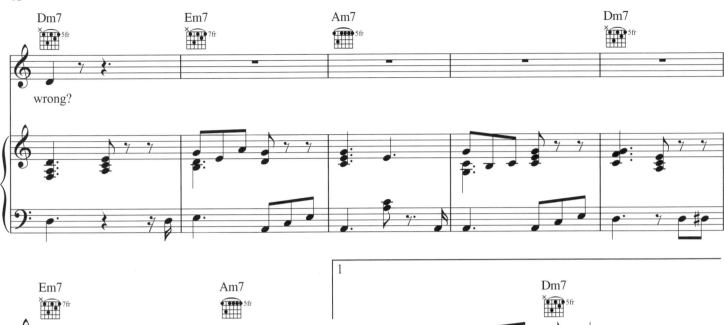

wrong?

Now, it's a long road,

but it's long-er with-out you. And with each pass-ing day,

I grow more un - cer - tain. Been a -

Meet me in the mid - dle, _____ tell me some - thing that could

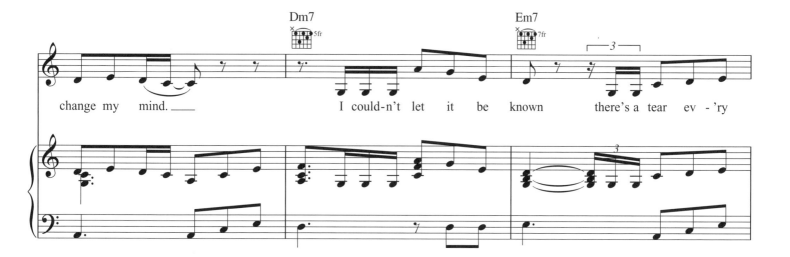

change my mind. _____ I could-n't let it be known there's a tear ev -'ry

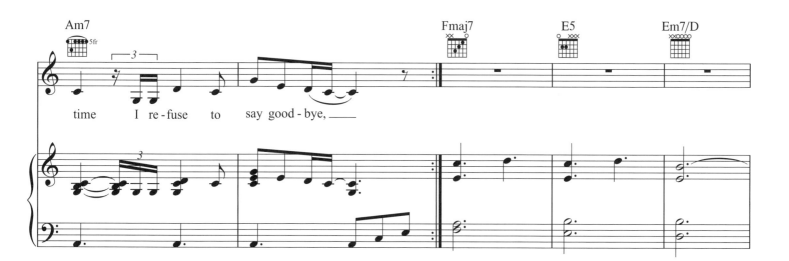

time I re - fuse to say good - bye, _____

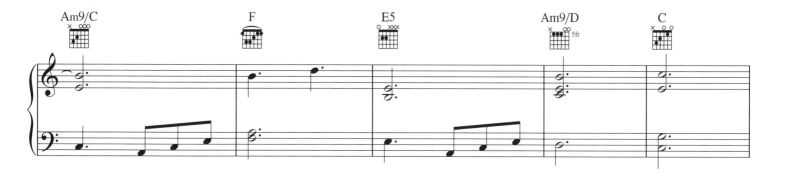

Meet me in the mid - dle, ___ tell me some - thing that could change my mind. ___ I could - n't let it be

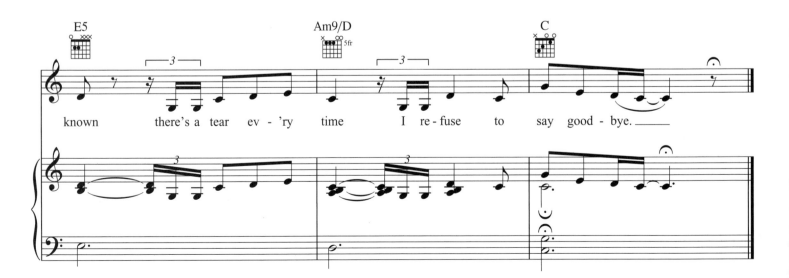

known there's a tear ev - 'ry time I re - fuse to say good - bye. ___

LOVE ME LIKE YOU DO

Words and Music by MAX MARTIN,
SAVAN KOTECHA, ILYA,
ALI PAYAMI and TOVE LO

Moderately slow

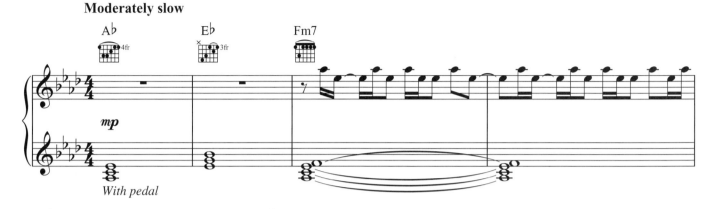

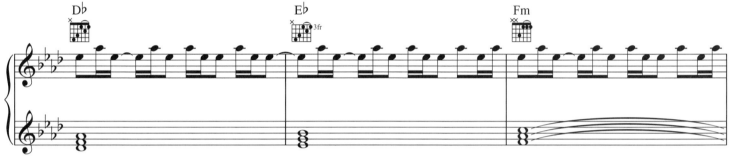

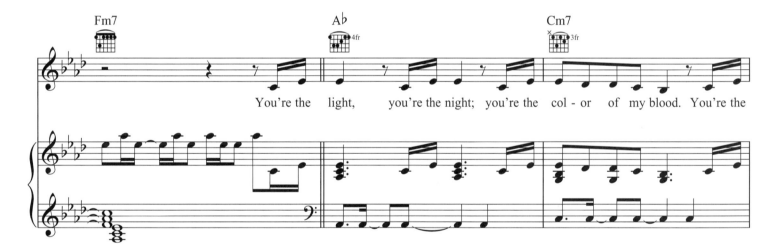

You're the light, you're the night; you're the col-or of my blood. You're the

cure, you're the pain; you're the on-ly thing I wan-na touch. ___ Nev-er

knew that it could mean so much, ___ so much. ___ You're the

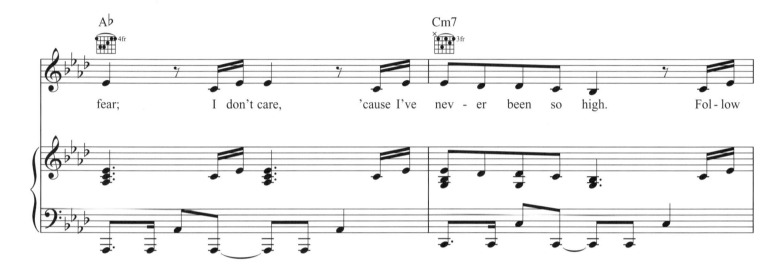

fear; I don't care, 'cause I've nev - er been so high. Fol - low

me through the dark; let me take you past, in - side the light. ___

You can see the world you brought to life, ___ to life. ___

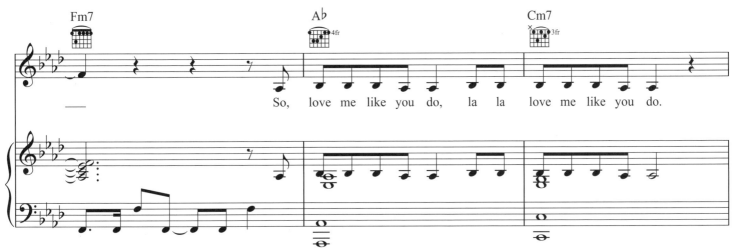

So, love me like you do, la la love me like you do.

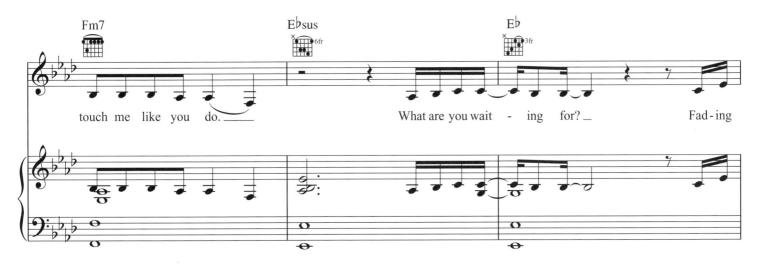

Love me like you do, la la love me like you do. Touch me like you do, ta ta

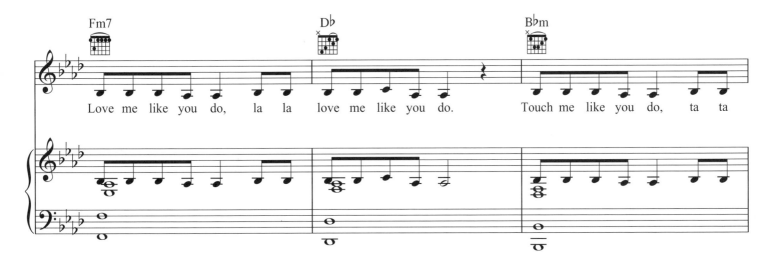

touch me like you do. _____ What are you wait - ing for? _ Fad - ing

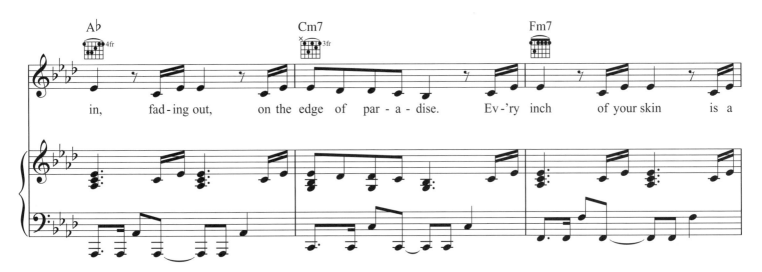

in, fad - ing out, on the edge of par - a - dise. Ev -'ry inch of your skin is a

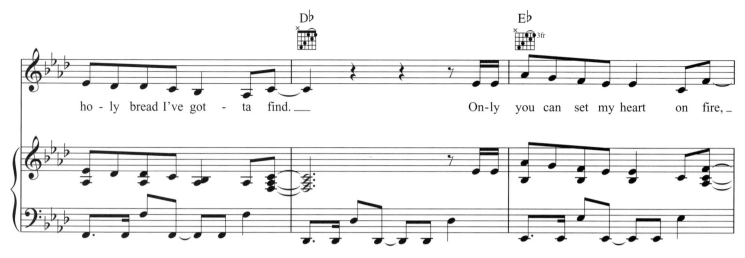

ho - ly bread I've got - ta find. ___ On-ly you can set my heart on fire, ___

___ on fire. ___ Yeah, I'll let you ___ set ___ the pace, ___

___ 'cause I'm not ___ think - ing straight. ___ My

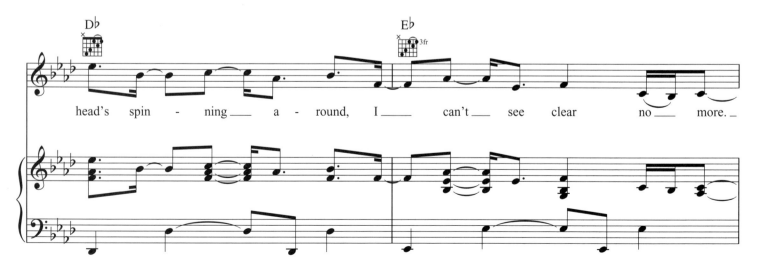

head's spin - ning ___ a - round, I ___ can't ___ see clear no ___ more. ___

What are you wait - ing for? ___

Love me like you do, la la love me like you do. Love me like you do, la la

love me like you do. Touch me like you do, ta ta touch me like you do. _____

What are you wait - ing for? ___

What are you wait - ing for? _____

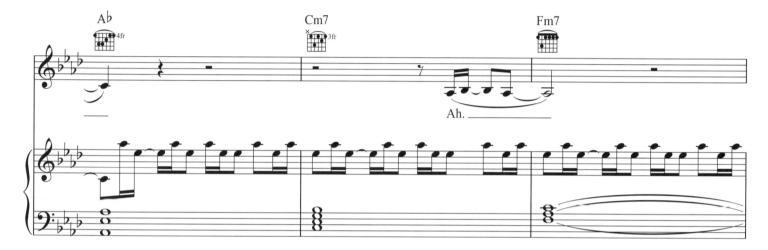

Ah. _____

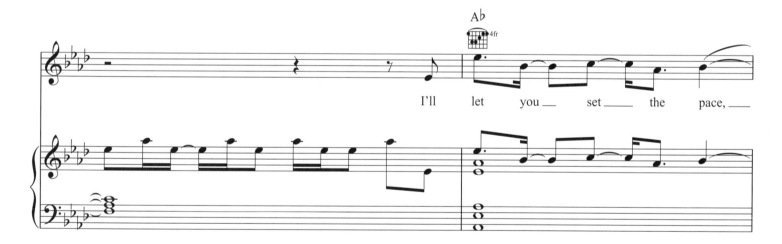

I'll let you _____ set _____ the pace, _____

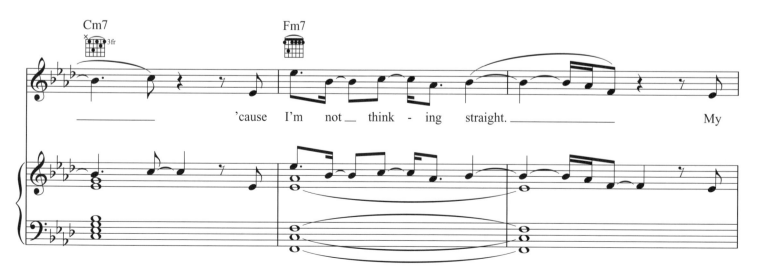

_____ 'cause I'm not _____ think - ing straight. _____ My

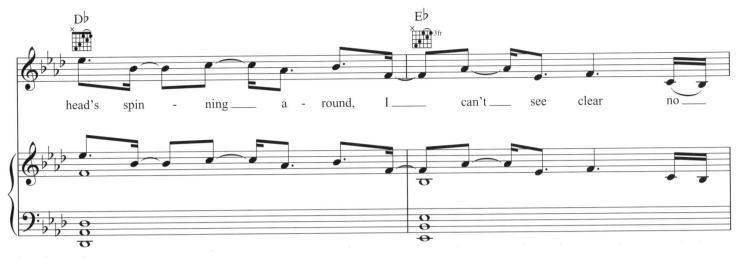

head's spin - ning ____ a - round, I ____ can't ____ see clear no ____

D.S. al Coda
(take repeat)

more. What are you wait - ing for? ____

CODA

What are you wait - ing for? _____

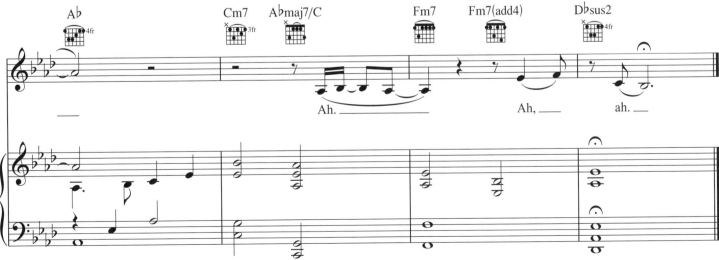

____ Ah. _____ Ah, ____ ah. ____

HAUNTED

Words and Music by BEYONCÉ KNOWLES
and BOOTS

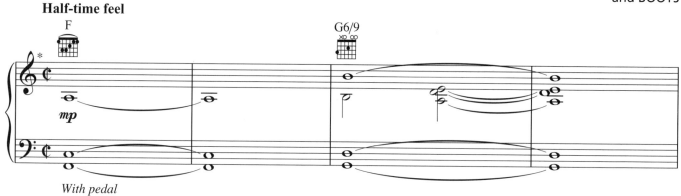

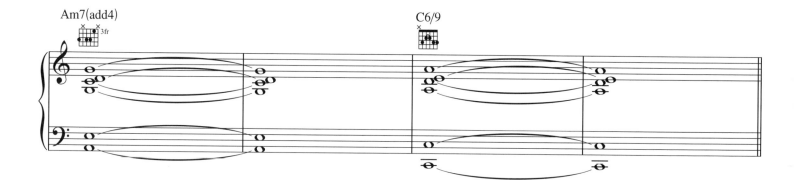

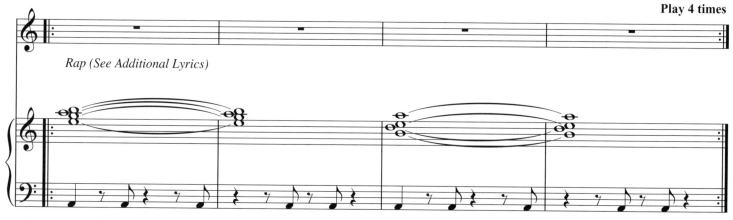

Rap (See Additional Lyrics)

Play 4 times

* *Recorded a half step lower.*

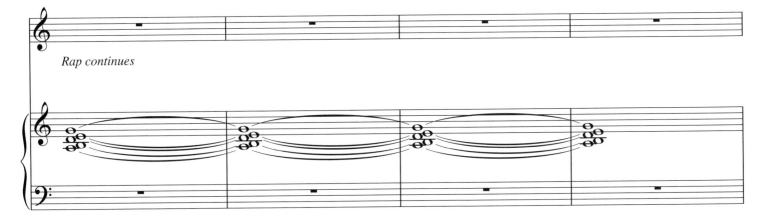

Rap continues

N.C.

Rap ends　　　　What goes　　　up _____　　　　　　　ghost　a - round, __

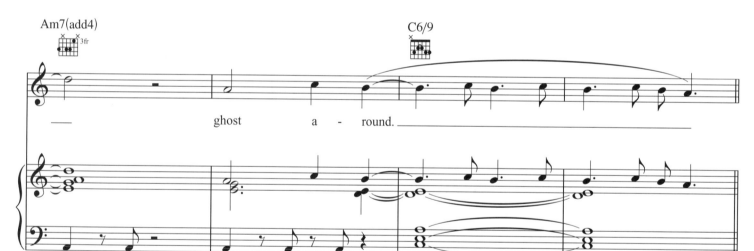

Spoken 1 (See additional lyrics)

(8vb)- -

loco

Slower

It's what you do, _____ it's what you see; _____

I know if I'm haunt-ing you, _____ you must _____ be haunt-ing me. _____

It's where we go, _____ it's where we'll be. _____

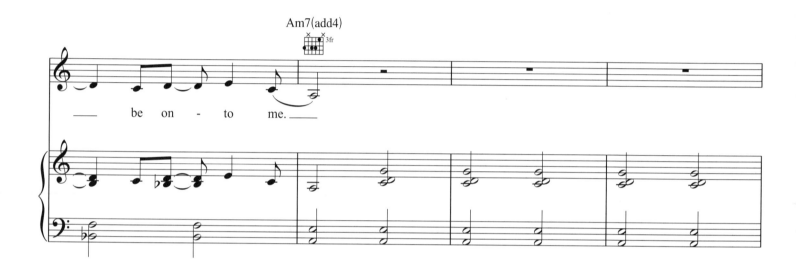

My wick-ed tongue, _ where will it be? ___

Fmaj13 Bb(add#4)

I know if I'm on - to you, _ I'm on - to you, _ on - to you, _ I'm on-

Fmaj13 Am7(add4)

- to you, _ on - to you, _ you must ___ be on - to me. ___

Spoken 2: (See additional lyrics)

N.C.

My haunt-ed lungs, ___   ghost in the sheets. ___

Spoken lyric ends

I know if I'm haunt-ing you, ___ you must ___ be haunt-ing me. ___

My wick-ed tongue, ___   where will it be? ___   I know if I'm

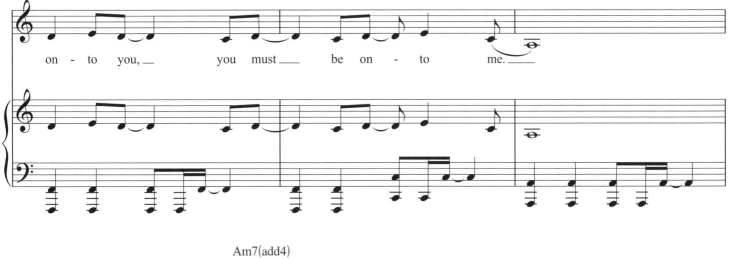

on - to you, ___ you must ___ be on - to me. ___

Am7(add4)

It's what we see; ___

N.C.

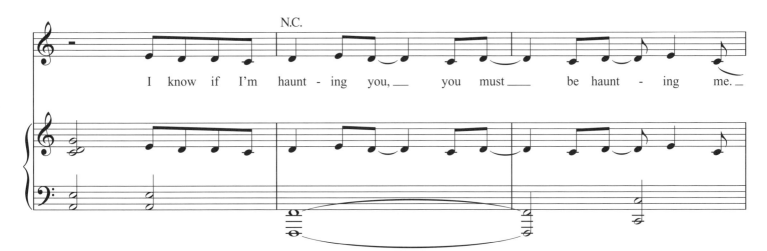

I know if I'm haunt - ing you, ___ you must ___ be haunt - ing me. ___

Am7(add4)

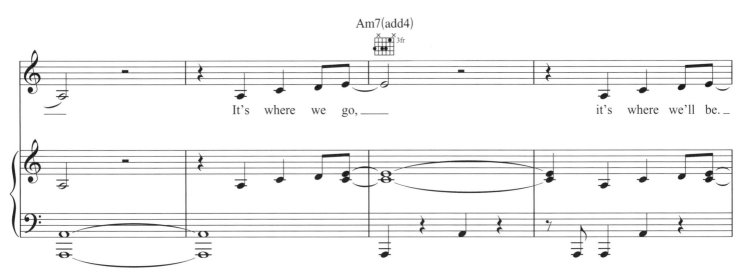

It's where we go, ___ it's where we'll be. ___

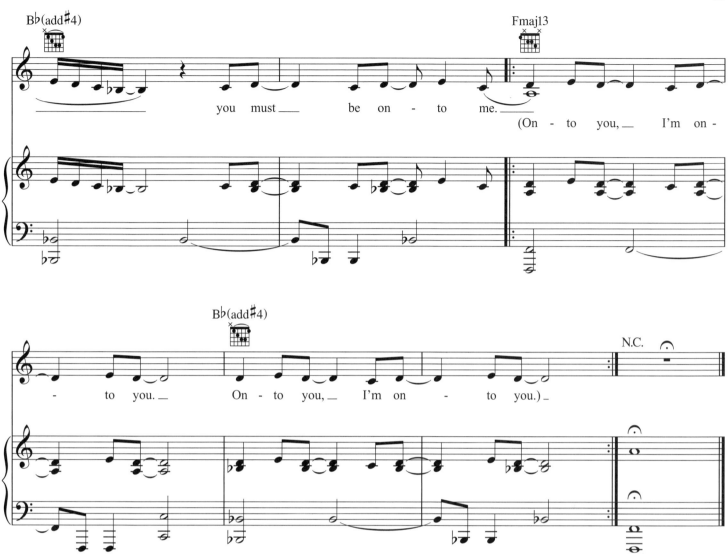

Additional Lyrics

Rap: And I've been drifting off on knowledge.
Cat-calls on cat-walks, man,
These women getting solemn.

I could sing a song for a Solomon or Salamander.
We took a flight at midnight,
And now my mind can't help but wander.
How come?

Spoon-fed pluralized eyes to find
The beaches in the forest.
When I'm looking off the edge, I preach my gut,

And can't help ignore it.
I'm climbing up the walls
'Cause all this shit I hear is boring.
All the shit I do is boring.
All these record labels, boring.

Rap continues: I don't trust these record labels, I'm torn.
All these people on the planet
Working 9 to 5, just to stay alive,
Then 9 to 5 just to stay alive,
Then 9 to 5 just to stay alive,
Then 9 to 5 just to stay alive,
And then 9 to 5 just to stay alive,

Then 9 to 5 just to stay alive,
Then 9 to 5 just to stay alive.
All the people on the planet
Working 9 to 5 just to stay alive.
How come?

Spoken 1: Soul not for sale.
Probably won't make no money off this...
Oh well.
Reap what you sow.
Perfection is so... Mm.

Spoken 2: You want me?
I walk down the hallway.
You're lucky;
The bedroom's our runway.

Slap me!
I'm pinned to the doorway.
Kiss, bite...
Foreplay.

SALTED WOUND

Words and Music by SIA FURLER,
BRIAN WEST, GERALD EATON
and OLIVER KRAUS

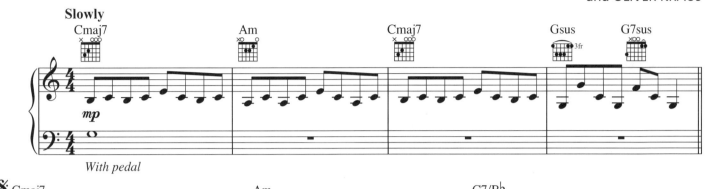

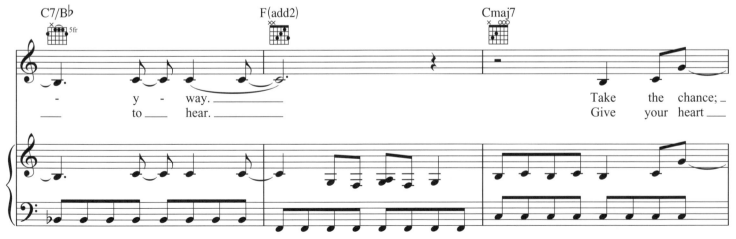

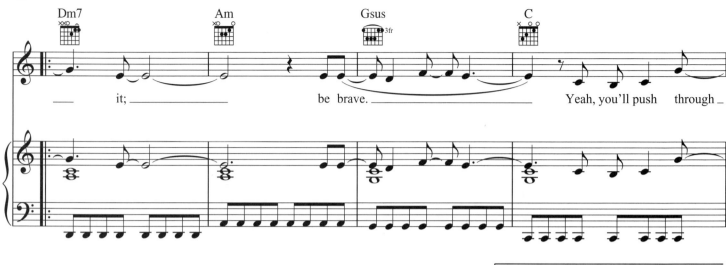

it; _____ be brave. _____ Yeah, you'll push through _

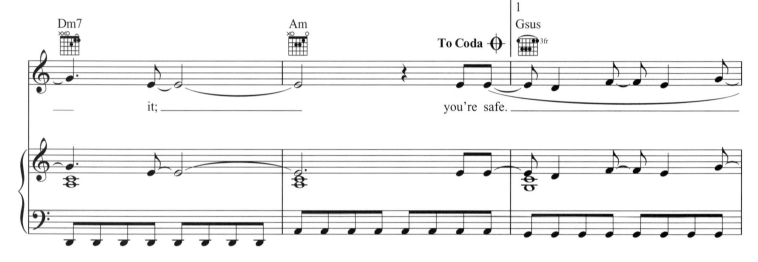

it; _____ you're safe. _____

Yes, you can do _ _____

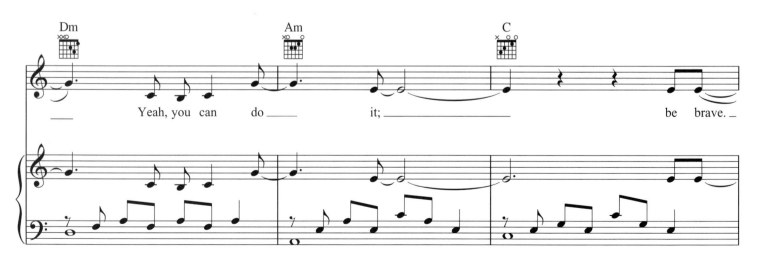

Yeah, you can do _____ it; _____ be brave. _

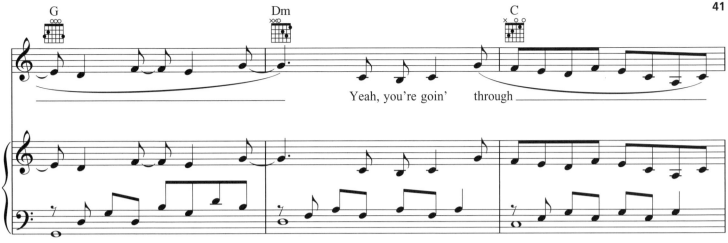

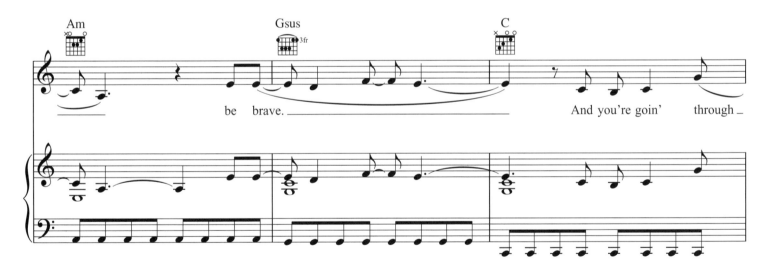

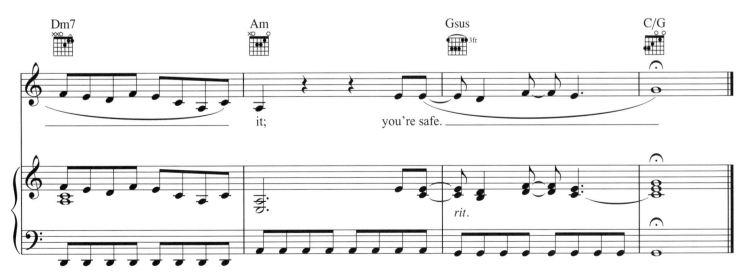

BEAST OF BURDEN

Words and Music by MICK JAGGER
and KEITH RICHARDS

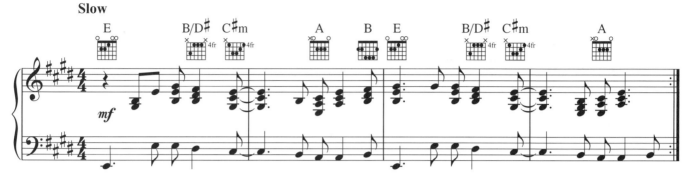

Slow

I'll nev-er be your Beast of Bur-den. My back is broad
I'll nev-er be your Beast of Bur-den. I've walked for miles;

but it's a-hurt-ing.
my feet are hurt-ing.

All I want is for you to make love to me.

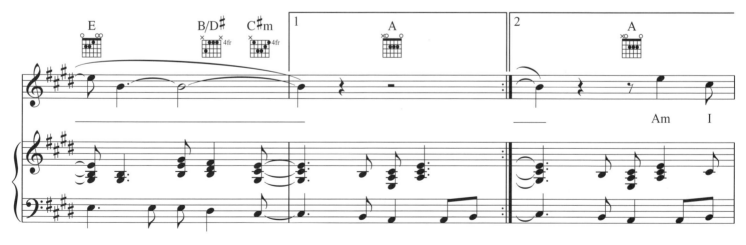

Am I

hard e - nough? __ Am I rough e - nough? __ Am I rich e - nough? __ I'm

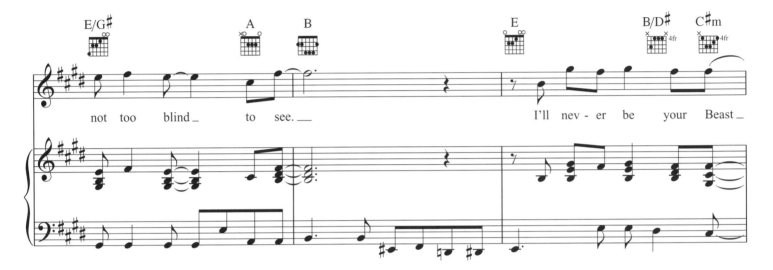

not too blind __ to see. __ I'll nev - er be your Beast __

__ of Bur - den. So, let's go home __ and draw the cur - tains.

Mu - sic on the ra - di - o, come on ba - by, make sweet love to me. __ Am I

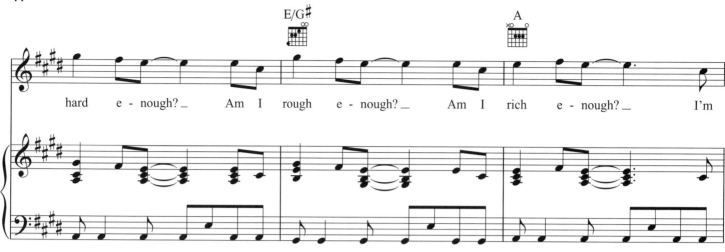

hard e - nough? _ Am I rough e - nough? _ Am I rich e - nough? _ I'm

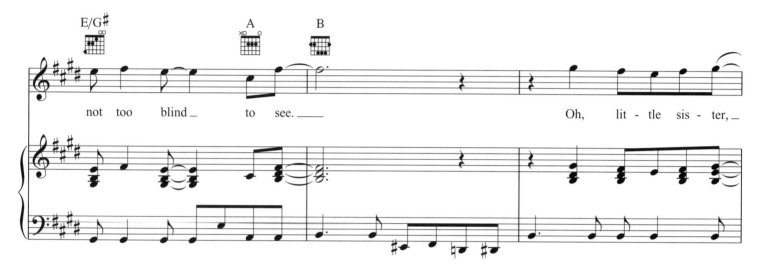

not too blind _ to see. ____ Oh, lit - tle sis - ter, _

____ pret - ty, pret - ty, pret - ty, pret - ty girl. _

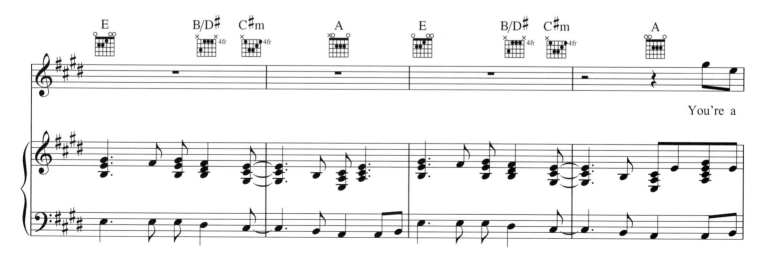

You're a

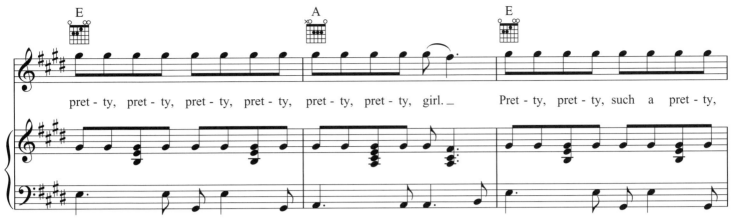

pret - ty, pret - ty, pret - ty, pret - ty, pret - ty, pret - ty, girl. __ Pret - ty, pret - ty, such a pret - ty,

pret - ty, pret - ty girl. __ Come on, ba - by, please, __ please, __ please.

(Spoken:) I'll tell ya, __ you can put me out on the street.

Put me out with no shoes on my feet, but *(Sung:)* put me out, put me out,

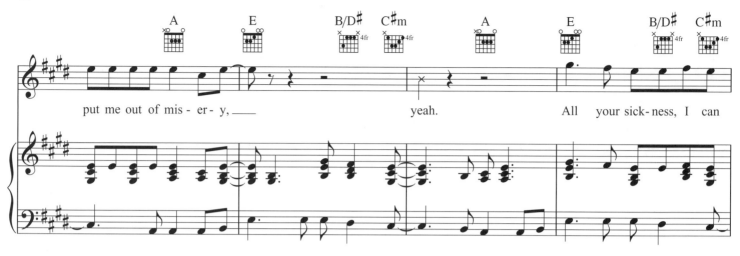

put me out of mis- er- y, ___ yeah. All your sick-ness, I can

suck it up. Throw it all at me, I can shrug it off.

There's one thing that I don't un - der - stand: you keep on tell - ing me I

ain't your kind of man. __ Ain't I rough e - nough? Oh! Ain't I

I'M ON FIRE

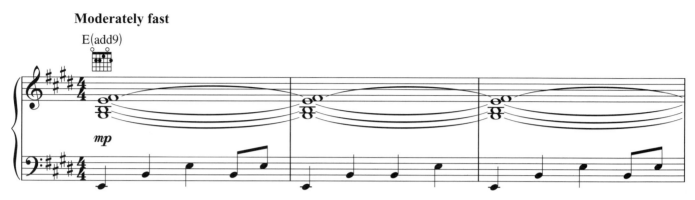

Words and Music by
BRUCE SPRINGSTEEN

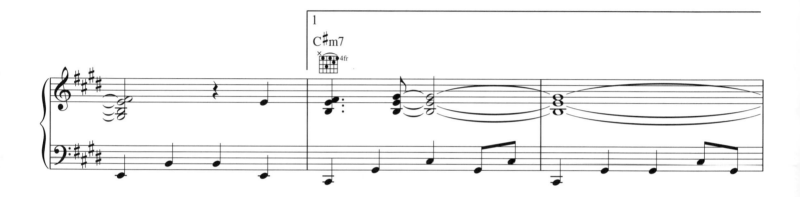

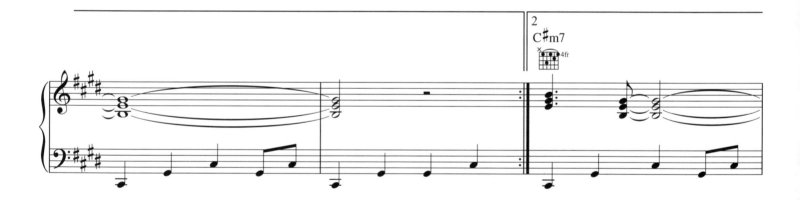

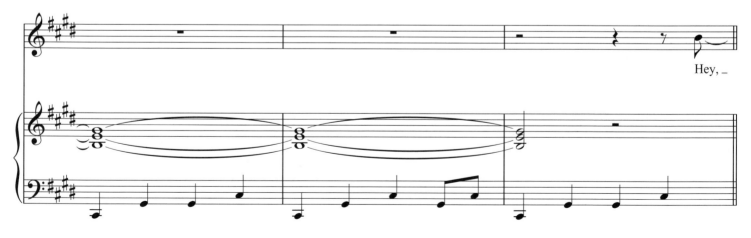

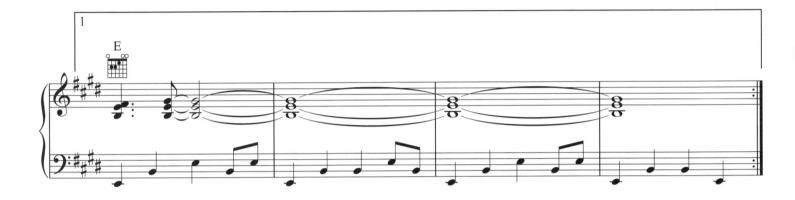

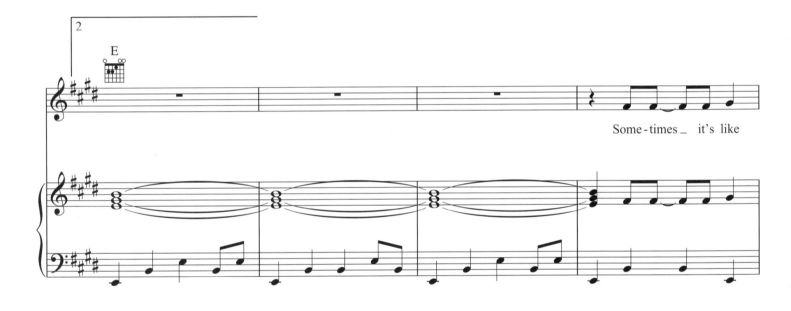

Some-times __ it's like

some-one took a knife, ba - by, ed - gy and dull, __ and cut a six - inch val - ley through the

D.S. al Coda

mid-dle of my soul.____ At night_

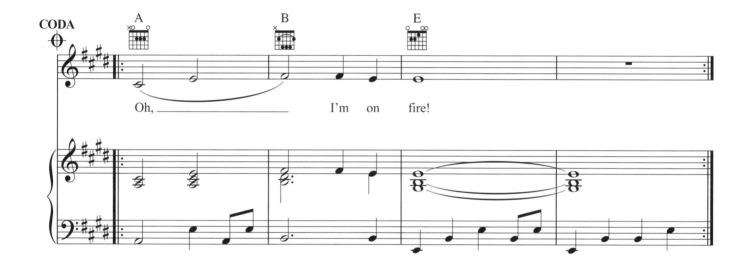

Oh,_____ I'm on fire!

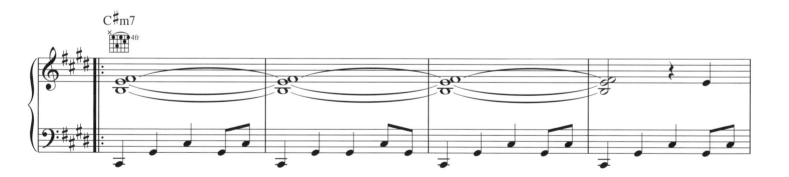

Repeat and Fade

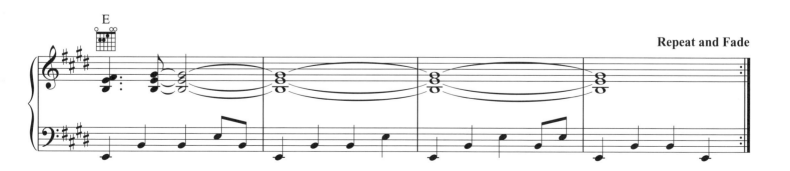

CRAZY IN LOVE
(2014 Remix)

Words and Music by BEYONCÉ KNOWLES,
RICH HARRISON, SEAN CARTER
and EUGENE RECORD

Moderately slow

Pedal ad lib. throughout

(Uh - oh, uh - oh, uh - uh, oh, no - no. Uh - oh, uh - oh, uh - oh, oh, no, no.

Uh - oh, uh - oh, uh - oh, oh, no, no. Uh - oh, uh - oh, oh - oh, oh, no, no.) You

got me look - ing ___ so cra - zy, my ba - by. I'm not my - self ___ late - ly, I'm

WITCHCRAFT

Music by CY COLEMAN
Lyrics by CAROLYN LEIGH

Medium bounce

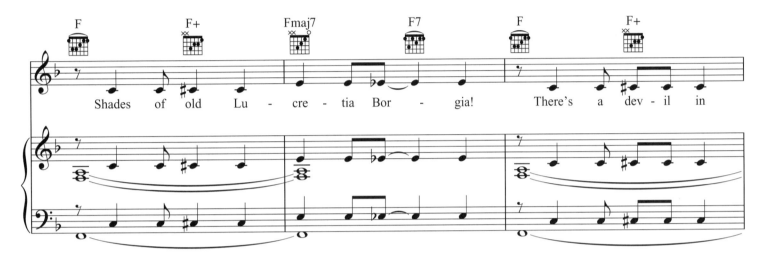

Shades of old Lu- cre- tia Bor- gia! There's a dev- il in

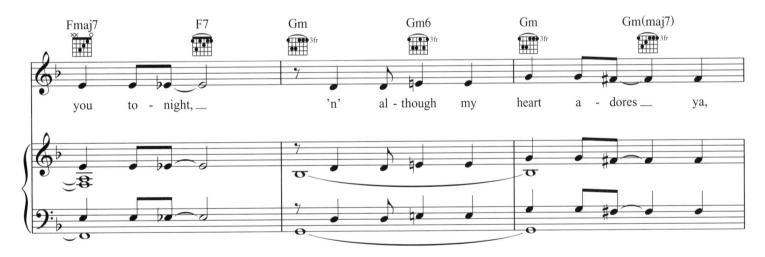

you to- night, __ 'n' al- though my heart a- dores __ ya,

my head says __ it ain't right, __ right to let you

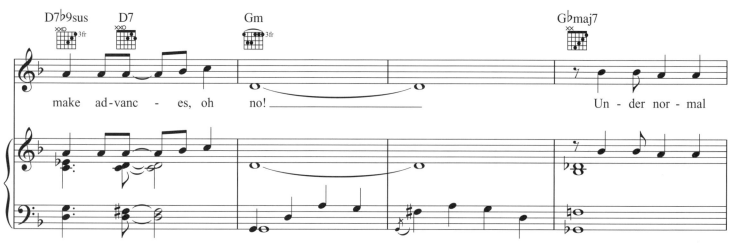

make ad-vanc - es, oh no! _____ Un - der nor - mal

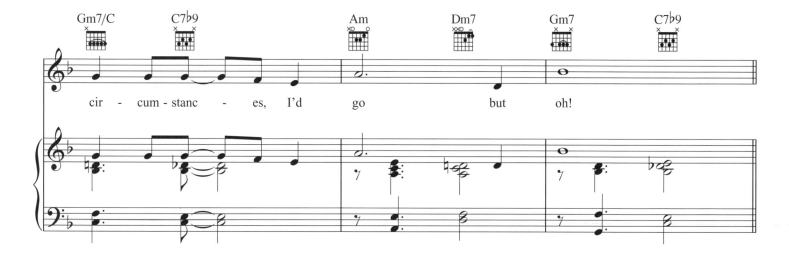

cir - cum - stanc - es, I'd go but oh!

Those fin - gers in my hair, ___ that sly, come -

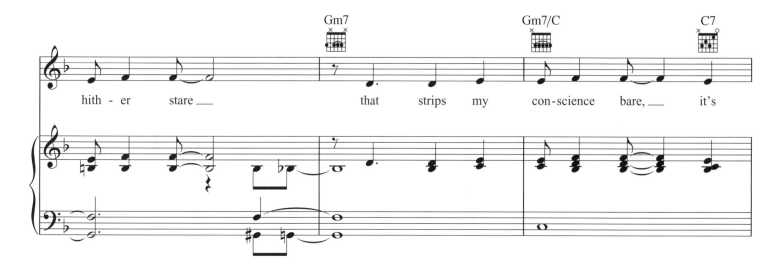

hith - er stare ___ that strips my con-science bare, ___ it's

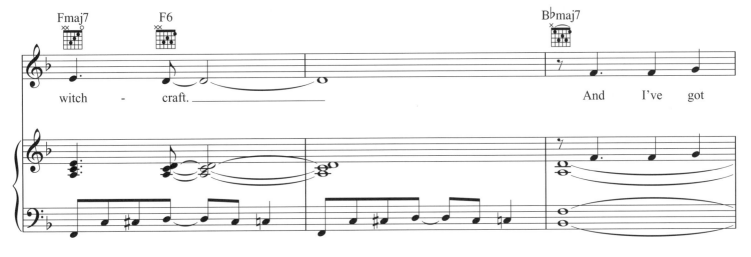

witch - craft. _____ And I've got

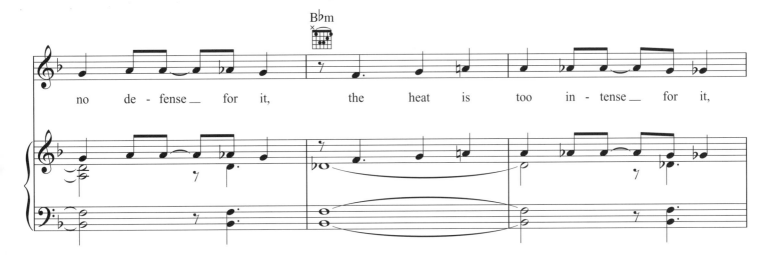

no de - fense _ for it, the heat is too in - tense _ for it,

what good would com - mon sense _ for it do? _____

_ 'Cause _ it's witch - craft! _ Wick - ed

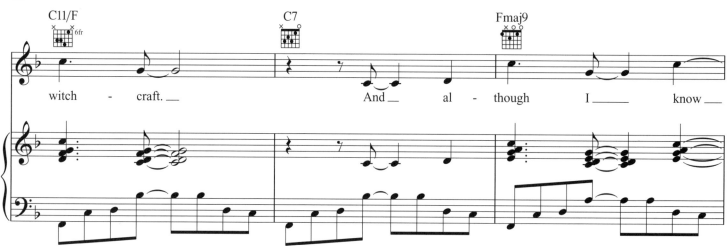

witch - craft. __ And __ al - though I ___ know ___

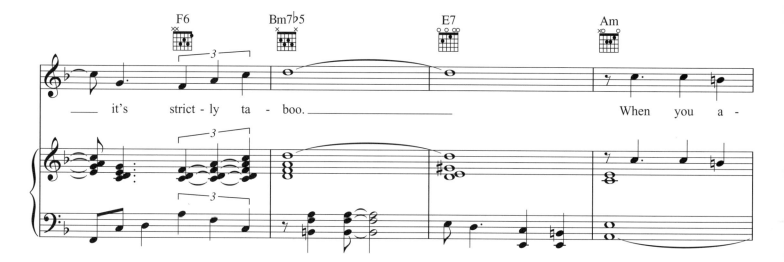

___ it's strict - ly ta - boo. _____ When you a -

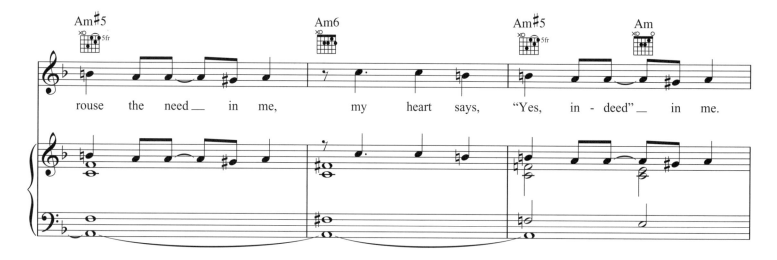

rouse the need __ in me, my heart says, "Yes, in - deed" __ in me.

"Pro - ceed with what you're lead - in' me to!" _____

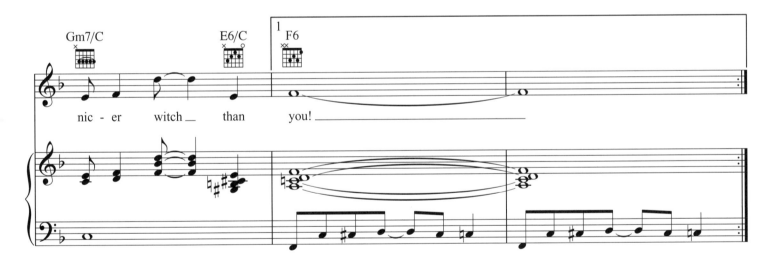

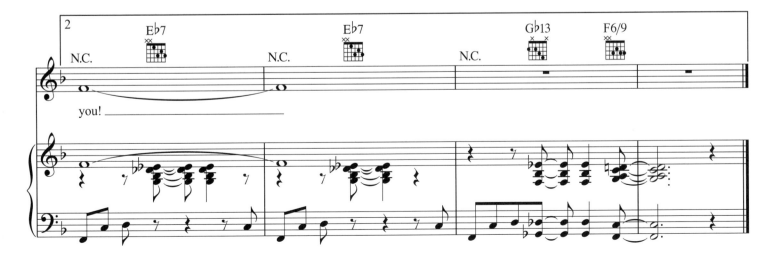

ONE LAST NIGHT

Words and Music by BARNABAS FREEMAN,
BENJAMIN VELLA and BLYTHE PEPINO

Recorded a half step higher.

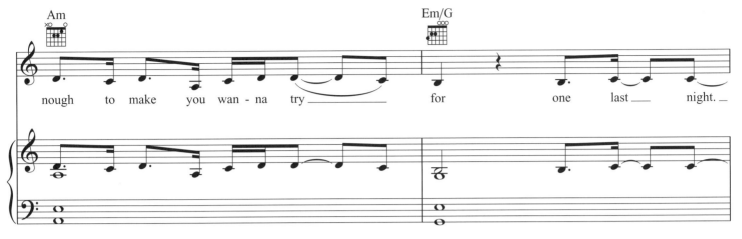

nough to make you wan - na try _____ for one last ___ night. __

Ghosts ___ and sil - hou - ettes... ___ they take a

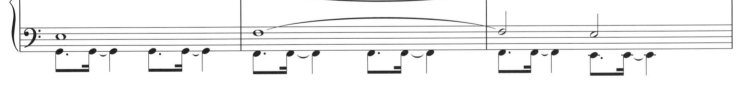

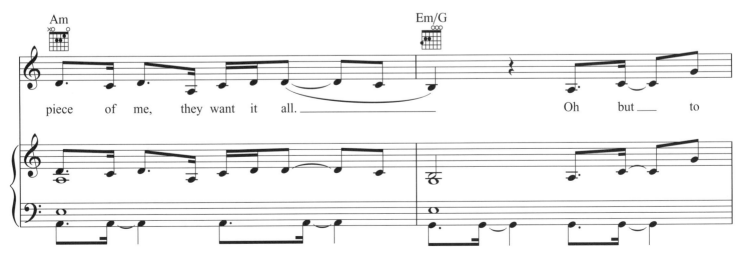

piece of me, they want it all. _____ Oh but ___ to

that we've been giv-en, _____ Let's live it like we care, _____ for one last night, _____

for one last night. _____

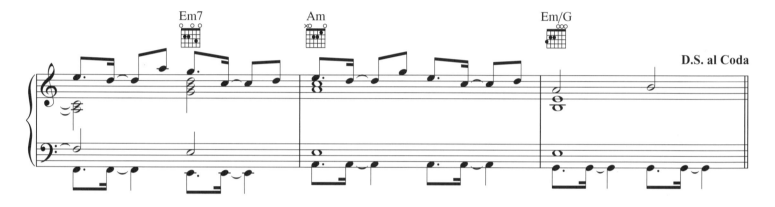

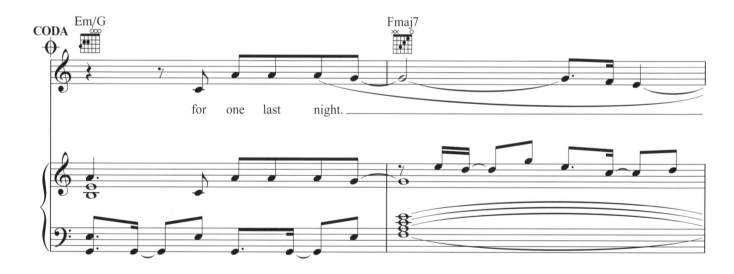

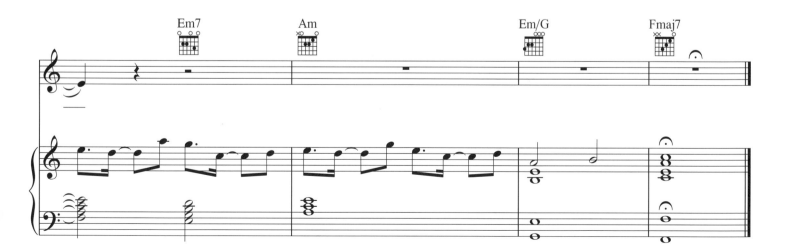

WHERE YOU BELONG

Words and Music by ABEL TESFAYE,
MIKE DEAN and AHMAD BALSHE

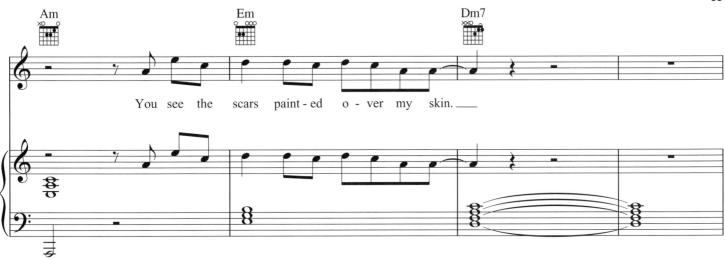

You see the scars paint-ed o-ver my skin.

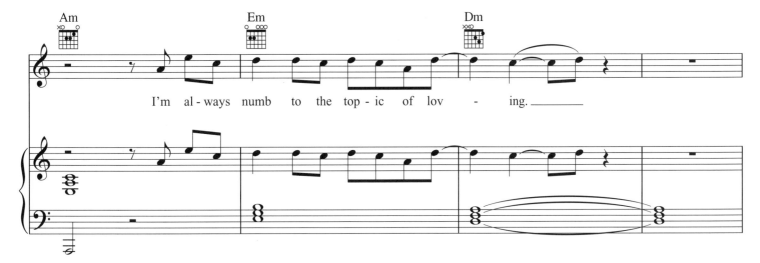

I'm al-ways numb to the top-ic of lov - ing.

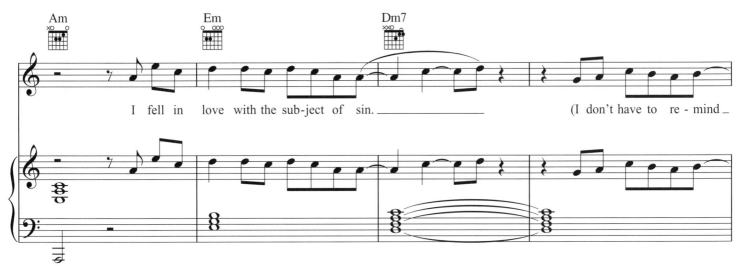

I fell in love with the sub-ject of sin. (I don't have to re-mind

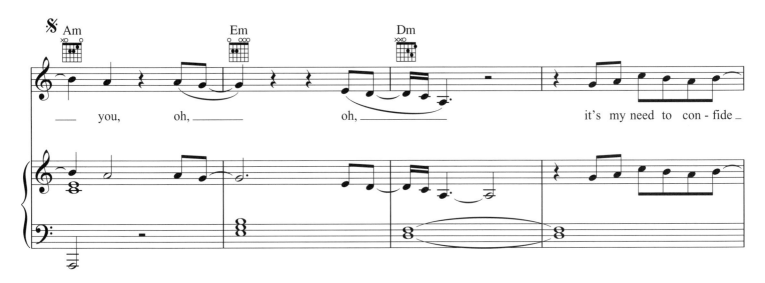

you, oh, oh, it's my need to con-fide

in you, oh, ___ oh. ___ I see your face ev-'ry time ___

___ I'm with some-bod - y else. Can't you see that I want ___ you? Put your feel-ings be-hind ___

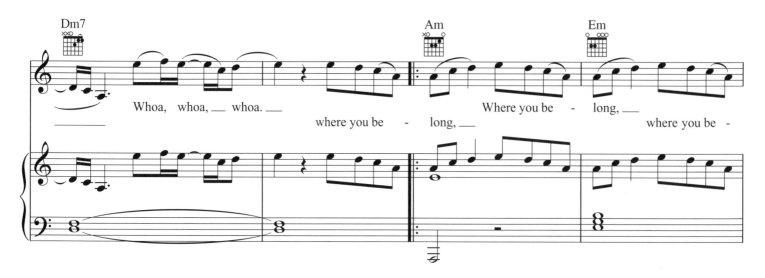

___ you. I don't have to re-mind ___ you, ooh. ___
I don't have to re-mind ___ you, oh, ___ oh, ___

Whoa, whoa, ___ whoa. ___ Where you be - long, ___
where you be - long, ___ where you be -

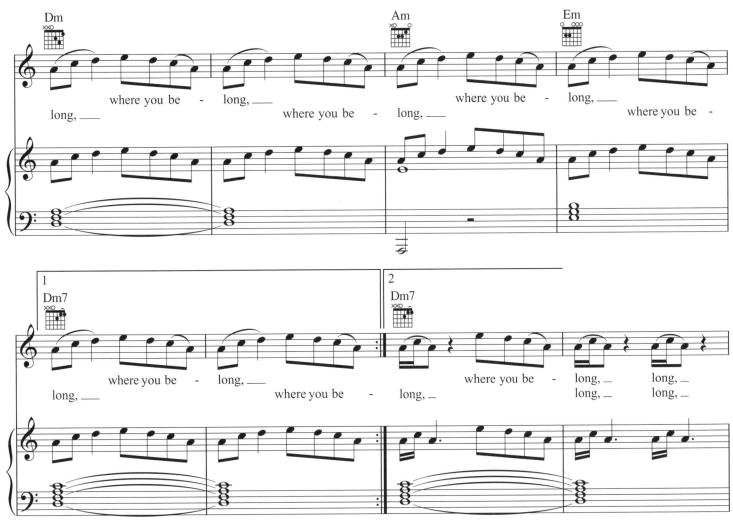

and I'm a leave a mark _ just to re-mind _ you where you be-long, _____ ba - by. _

Give me your all, scream as loud as you want. _____

D.S. al Coda

(I don't have to re-mind _

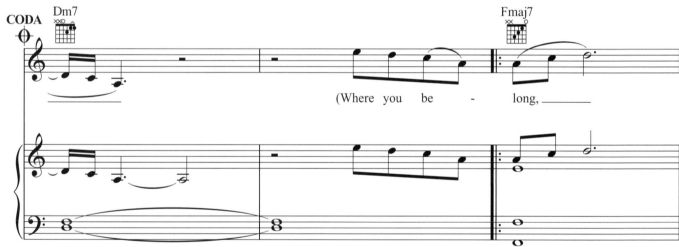

CODA

(Where you be - long, _____

where you be - long, _____ where you be - long, _____

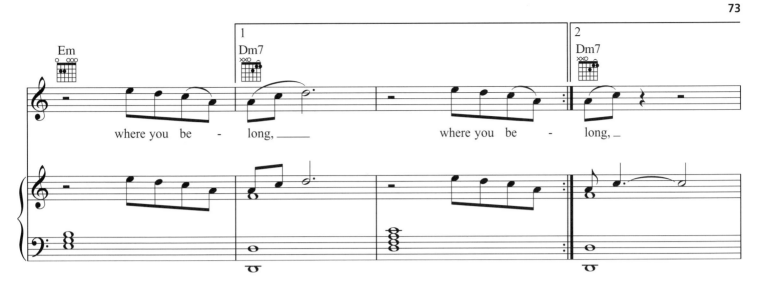

where you be - long, ____ where you be - long, __

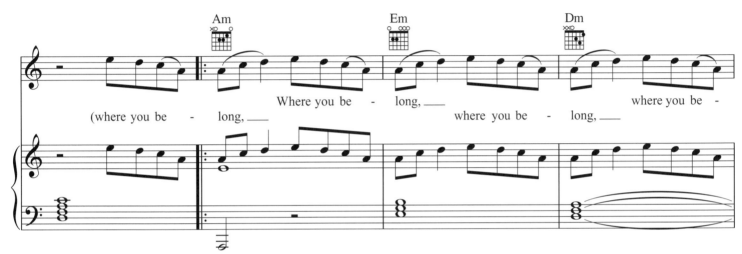

Where you be - long, ____ where you be - long, ____ where you be -

(where you be - long, ____

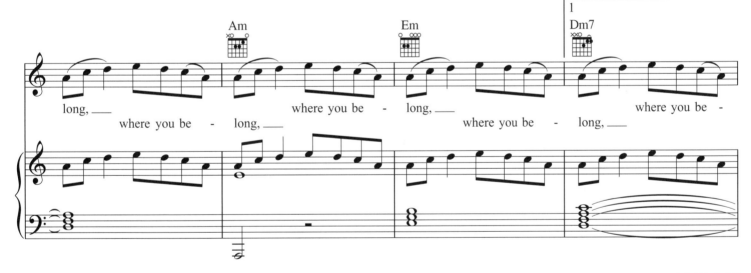

long, ____ where you be - long, ____ where you be - long, ____ where you be -

where you be - long, ____ where you be - long, ____

long, ____ where you be - long, __ long, __ long.

where you be - long, __ long, __ long, __ long.)

I KNOW YOU

Words and Music by SKYLAR GREY
and STEPHAN MOCCIO

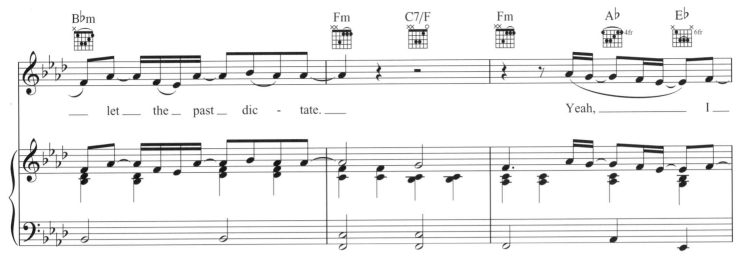

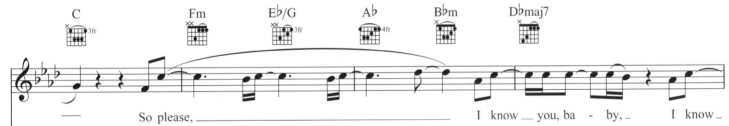

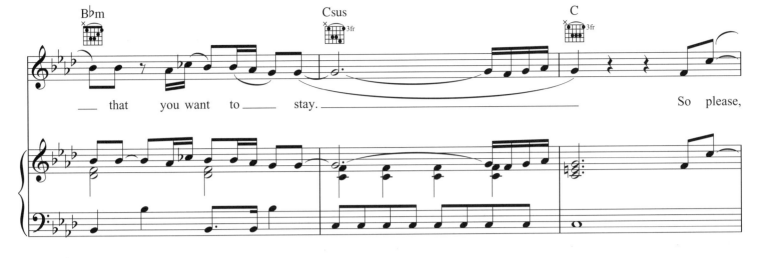

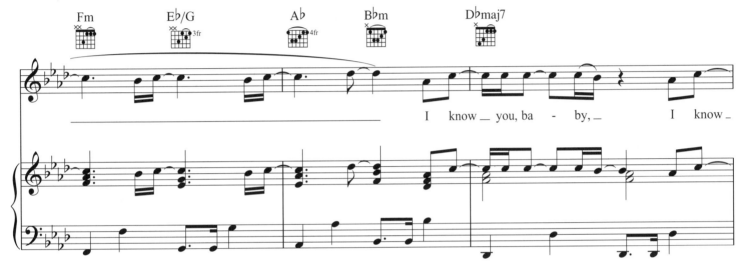

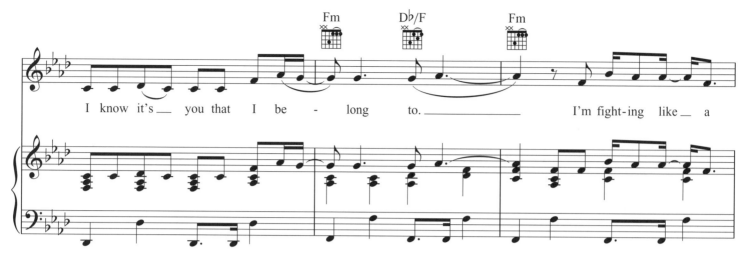

I know it's ___ you that I be - long to. _____ I'm fight-ing like ___ a

cann - on - ball ___ in the air, crash-ing in - to who I be - long ___ to.

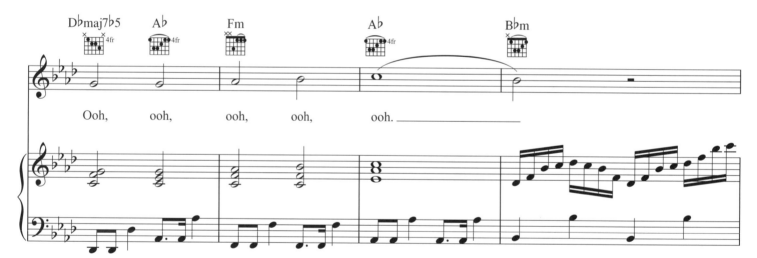

Ooh, ooh, ooh, ooh, ooh. _____

I ___ have _ been _ pa - tient but slow - ly I'm los - in' ___ faith. _

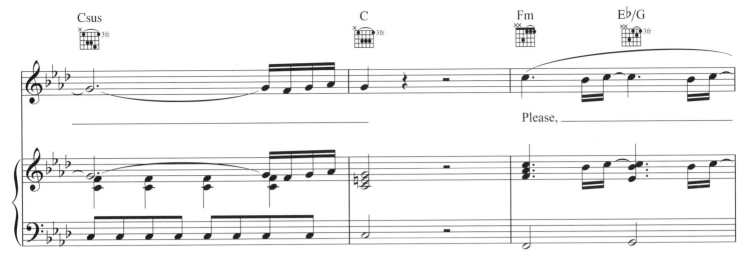

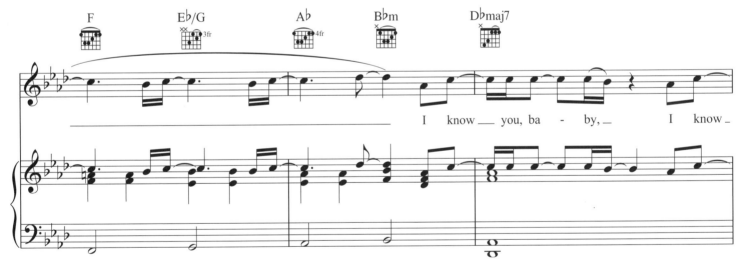

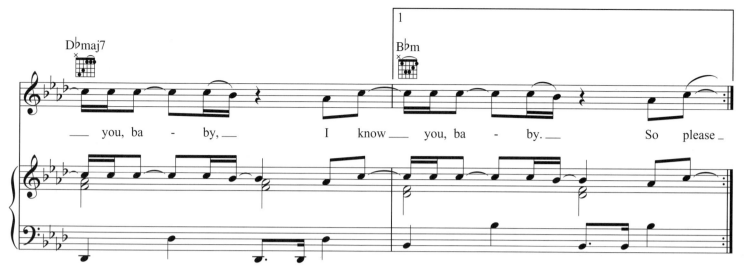

you, ba - by, __ I know __ you, ba - by. __ So please __

__ you, ba - by. __ The sha - dows __ of __ your __ heart are hang-in' __ in __ the __ sheets, wait-ing, __

__ wait - ing. __ I know __ you, ba - by. __ The se - crets __ that __ you __ hide come

drown __ us and __ it's just like, ba - by. __ I know __ you, ba - by. __